YOUR KNOWLEDGE HAS VALUE

- We will publish your bachelor's and master's thesis, essays and papers

- Your own eBook and book - sold worldwide in all relevant shops

- Earn money with each sale

Upload your text at www.GRIN.com
and publish for free

Bibliographic information published by the German National Library:

The German National Library lists this publication in the National Bibliography; detailed bibliographic data are available on the Internet at http://dnb.dnb.de .

This book is copyright material and must not be copied, reproduced, transferred, distributed, leased, licensed or publicly performed or used in any way except as specifically permitted in writing by the publishers, as allowed under the terms and conditions under which it was purchased or as strictly permitted by applicable copyright law. Any unauthorized distribution or use of this text may be a direct infringement of the author s and publisher s rights and those responsible may be liable in law accordingly.

Imprint:

Copyright © 2011 GRIN Verlag
Print and binding: Books on Demand GmbH, Norderstedt Germany
ISBN: 9783668639218

This book at GRIN:

https://www.grin.com/document/412703

Longji Ayuba Dachal

Truth and Freedom in the Gospels. The Book of Luke

GRIN Verlag

GRIN - Your knowledge has value

Since its foundation in 1998, GRIN has specialized in publishing academic texts by students, college teachers and other academics as e-book and printed book. The website www.grin.com is an ideal platform for presenting term papers, final papers, scientific essays, dissertations and specialist books.

Visit us on the internet:

http://www.grin.com/

http://www.facebook.com/grincom

http://www.twitter.com/grin_com

TRUTHS AND FREEDOM IN THE GOSPELS: THE BOOK OF LUKE

BY LONGJI AYUBA DACHAL

Table of contents

I. Introduction
II. Analysis of the book of Luke
    i. Structure of the book of Luke
    ii. Message
        a. Theme
        b. Anticipated reader response
    iii. Argument
        a. Theme development
        b. Anticipated reader response
III. Background of the book of Luke
IV. Conclusion

Introduction

If two people who have been living in Nassarawa Gwom, a community in Jos North Local Government Area of Plateau state, Nigeria who have been eye witnesses to any of the Jos crisis are asked to give a report or the story of what they saw and experienced, their story will mostly be similar but with more emphasis and details to events that interest them the most or affects them the most either negative or positive. This was somewhat the scenario of the writers of the synoptic gospels in some sense. Mark and Matthew were Jews, so their gospels, which were written for a Jewish audience reflects the Jewish worldview, Jewish perspectives, style of writing, and a more detail explanation of beliefs, practices and values of the Jews, etc.

Luke was a gentile; his style of writing too reflected the gentile worldview, beliefs, practices and values targeted at the gentile audience. For example, to the Jew, a person's family line or genealogy determines his/her identity (genuity, respect and dignity). The Jews also trace their genealogy to Abraham, who was the founder of the Jewish nation. This justifies why Matthew began his writing with the genealogy of Jesus, tracing Jesus' line to David (to show a fulfillment of the OT prophecies that the messiah will descent from the line of David) and to Abraham (who is the father of the Jews, to show that Jesus was related to al the Jews). The gentiles on the other hand believed that Adam is the father of all human beings. This is evident in Luke's gospel; he was a gentile, writing from a gentile perspective, he traced the genealogy of Jesus to Adam. This was to show that "Jesus is related to all human beings. This is consistent with Luke's picture of Jesus as the savior of the whole world."[1]

The similarities of the gospel accounts are without differences, there are events that are captured in one account that is not captured in the other. There are instances where Matthew agrees with Luke against Mark. The differences are considered as the synoptic problem but this paper will not delve into the debates concerning that.

---

[1] Ronald A. Beers (Ed.), *New Living Translation Life Application Study Bible*. Carol Steam, Illinois, Tyndale House Publishers, Inc., 2007: 1682.

Analysis of the Book of Luke
Structure of the book of Luke

From my readings of the book of Luke, I see the main structure of the book of Luke divided into four: Jesus' early life Chap. 1:1-4:13, the ministry of Jesus in Galilee 4:14-9:50, Jesus' ministry on his way from Galilee to Jerusalem 9:51-19:27, Jesus' ministry in Jerusalem where he was eventually betrayed, died, resurrected and ascended into heaven 19:28-24:53. But for the purpose of this research, I have adopted the detailed outline for the book of Luke as presented by John A. Martin:

I. The Prologue and Purpose of the Gospel (1:1-4)

II. The Births and Maturations of John and Jesus (1:5-2:52)
  A. The announcements of the births (1:5-56)
  B. The births and boyhoods of John and Jesus (1:57-2:52)

III. The Preparation for Jesus' Ministry (3:1-4:13)
  A. The ministry of John the Baptist (3:1-20)
  B. The baptism of Jesus (3:21-22)
  C. The genealogy of Jesus (3:23-38)
  D. The temptation of Jesus (4:1-13)

IV. The Ministry of Jesus in Galilee (4:14-9:50)
  A. The initiation of Jesus' ministry (4:14-30)
  B. The authentication of Jesus' authority (4:31-6:16)
  C. Jesus' sermon on the level place (6:17-49)
  D. Jesus' ministry in Capernaum and surrounding cities (chaps. 7-8)
  E. Jesus' teaching of His disciples (9:1-50)

V. The Journey of Jesus toward Jerusalem (9:51-19:27)
  A. The rejection of Jesus by most on His journey toward Jerusalem (9:51-11:54)
  B. Jesus' teaching of His followers in view of the rejection (12:1-19:27)

VI. The Ministry of Jesus in Jerusalem (19:28-21:38)
  A. Jesus' entry into Jerusalem as Messiah (19:28-44)
  B. Jesus in the temple (19:45-21:38)

VII. The Death, Burial, and Resurrection of Jesus (chaps. 22-24)

A. The death and burial of Jesus (chaps. 22-23)
B. The resurrection and appearances of Jesus (chap. 24)[2]

Message

Theme: Jesus came to save the lost

Anticipated Reader Response: Repent, believed and be saved.

Key verse: Luke 19:9-10. Jesus said to him, "Today salvation has come to this house, because this man, too, is a son of Abraham. For the Son of Man came to seek and to save what was lost." NIV

Key text: Luke 5:27-32. After this, Jesus went out and saw a tax collector by the name of Levi sitting at his tax booth. "Follow me," Jesus said to him, and Levi got up, left everything and followed him. Then Levi held a great banquet for Jesus at his house, and a large crowd of tax collectors and others were eating with them. But the Pharisees and the teachers of the law who belonged to their sect complained to his disciples, "Why do you eat and drink with tax collectors and 'sinners'?" Jesus answered them, "It is not the healthy who need a doctor, but the sick. I have not come to call the righteous, but sinners to repentance." NIV

Argument

Theme Development

i. Truth and salvation: Luke was not a Jew, meaning that he was a gentile as the Jews might have called him. Writing probably for the gentiles though he wrote to Theophilus. He presented salvation in Christ Jesus open to people from every part of the world. Luke sees everybody, regardless of ethnicity and race as included in the scope of salvation. He thus presented the message of the angels to the shepherds as good news of 'peace on earth' and a goodwill to men (2:14), not simply peace in Israel and goodwill to the Jews. Leon Morris observes that "it is significant that both he [Luke] and Matthew quote from Isaiah 40 in connection

---

[2] John A. Martin, "Luke," in the *Bible Knowledge Commentary: New Testament*.(eds., Walvoord, John F. and Zuck, Roy B.), Cook communications ministries, 2000. Accessed through the PC Study Bible, version 5.

with the ministry of john the Baptist. But where Matthew has three lines of prophecy, enough to tell of the voice calling on people to prepare the way of the Lord, Luke adds another five until he comes to the words 'all flesh will see God's salvation' 3:4-6"[3]

Luke's gospel and his other account in the book of Acts of the Apostles presented and emphasized in details and more of women, children, the poor, the disreputable and worst of all the Samaritans. All of the above listed were regarded as nothing, inferior, outcast and without dignity in the Jewish culture and contexts which the gospels of Mark and Matthew gave no or less details and considerations to. Unlike in Rome, before and during Jesus' time on earth, women, especially those of the upper class had freedom compared to women in the Greek and Jewish culture and contexts. The Jewish culture sees women as inferior to men, jewish women were arraigned alongside the slaves, deaf, mutes, the binds etc. they are considered not eligible to lay hands on an animal to be sacrificed, and they are also not eligible to give witness or evidence in the courts. They are excluded from being disciples to Rabbis; the Rabbis regarded teaching women as a sin. Leon Morris submitted that as far as a Jew is concern, "if any man gives his daughter a knowledge of the law it is as though he taught her lechery (Mishnah, *Sotah* 3:4). There is a very old prayer that a man might pray: 'Blessed art thou, O Lord ... who hast not made me a woman'."[4] In the Greek culture on the other hand, women have no rights and freedom, they belong to their husbands. If they become widows, they belong to their sons, suitors are arranged for them, and they are not allowed to own property of their own etc.

Luke included more women and gave more detailed information of them than the other gospels did. He begins his account with a long narrative of the infancy of John the Baptist and Jesus where he presented Elizabeth and Mary as the subjext of the narrative. He also included the song of Mary 1:46-55, he included the comment of prophetess Anna concerning the fate of Jesus. He also mentions the women in Jesus' entourage by name 8:1-3, and many instances where Jesus encountered women more detailed than the other gospels. He

---

[3] Leon Morris, *New Testament Theology,* Grand Rapids, Michigan, Zondervan Publishing House, 1990:200.
[4] Morris, *New Testament Theology,* Grand Rapids, Michigan, Zondervan Publishing House, 1990:202.

presented Jesus' ministry as including the poor when he used the word poor ten times against Mark and Matthew who both used the word fives. Luke also has various accounts that involved the outcast. Out of the 21 appearances of tax collectors, Luke has ten. Luke also presented several of Jesus' parables where the outcasts were the central figure 18:9-14, 7:41-42; 12:13-21; 15:11-32; 16:1-12; 18:1-8.

Luke knew that the gentiles possessing gentile blood cannot attain righteousness based on the Jewish laws, so in his gospel, he focused his reportage concisely and vividly on Jesus' contact with those considered rejected and outcasts. Morris observed that Luke's gospel was not "concerned with conventional patterns of righteousness. He was well aware that Jesus was concerned with saving sinful people from their sins and that he was often found with those whom the religious leaders of his day would have condemned and rejected. But that is not the Christian way. Luke lets us see that there is hope for the worst and most despised people. The followers of Jesus should despair of no one."[5]

ii. Truth about forgiveness of sins: many sinners who were regarded outcast got their sins forgiven by God when they exercised faith in him and his healing power, 5:20 etc. All that had faith in Jesus, regardless of their races, statutes, or ethnicity all had their sins forgiven. Luke gave record of more people who were not Jews but were healed because of their faith. Luke portrayed the fact that faith is the basis of salvation in the new covenant, and he presented people who were considered not beneficiaries of God's redemptive plans by the law and the Jews as beneficiaries of salvation in the new covenant on the basis of their faith.

Anticipated Reader Response (ARR)

i. The truth about salvation leads to freedom from the bondage of sin and result in the response of the believer through prayer, rejoicing and offering praises to God. Leon Morris commented that "sometimes Christianity has been presented as a very serious faith, solemn to the point of being gloomy. People have been so set

---

[5] Morris, *New Testament Theology*, 211.

on attaining the joys of heaven that they have forgotten the joys of earth, Luke would not have recognized such a way as truly Christian. Joy runs through his two volumes…"[6] The scenario surrounding the birth of john the Baptist and Jesus Christ incited joys and praises from Mary, Zachariah and Elizabeth. The birth of Christ who was to bring salvation to mankind alone sets many people free. Zachariah and Elizabeth were without a child, they endured through the pains of being childless, the angel who announced the birth of john the Baptist inform Zachariah that: "you will have joy and gladness and many will rejoice at his birth" (1:14). The birth really brought joy to the family and neighbors. Luke 1:57-58 "When it was time for Elizabeth to have her baby, she gave birth to a son. 58 Her neighbors and relatives heard that the Lord had shown her great mercy, and they shared her joy."NIV The birth of John the Baptist also resulted in Zachariah gaining his ability to speak again. Mary sang song of praises to God, "my spirit rejoices in God my savior" (1:47) when she was told that she carried the messiah in her womb. At the birth of Jesus Christ, the angels rejoiced and sang praises to God (2:13-14) and then followed by the shepherds (2:20).

The lame man who was healed by Jesus responded by glorifying God so also the people who saw him healed (5:25-260). The healing of the son of the widow of Nain resulted in glorifying and praising God 7:16, the blind who was healed on the way of Jericho, the leper who was cleansed all rejoiced and praised God.

ii. The truth about the forgiveness of sins demands repentance from people, which will set them free from the wrath of God and God's punishment of sinners: all the NT writers made a clarion call to sinners in one way or the other to repent from their sins. Out of the numerous calls for repentance, Luke stressed and emphasized the need for repentance more than the other NT writers. For example, the Greek verbs *metanoia* and *metanoeo* means "change of direction, conversion, repentance and turn around, change one's mind, repent"[7] respectively.

The verb *metanoia* occurred 8 times in the synoptic gospels, 5 of the occurrences were from the book of Luke. It appeared once and twice in the

---

[6] Morris, *New Testament Theology*, 1990: 214.
[7] Horst Balz and Gerhard Schneider (ed), *Exegetical Dictionary of the New Testament.* Grand Rapids, Michigan, William B. Eerdmans Publishing Company,©1990. All rights reserved. Accessed through the PC Study Bible, version 5.

gospels of Mark and Matthew respectively. The verb *metavoeo* appeared 22 times in the New Testament. But Luke, according to Leon Morris, "thus has 11 of the 22 New Testament occurrences of the word"[8] (including its six appearances in the book of Acts which Luke happens to be the author). *metanoeo* appeared twice in Mark, five times in Matthew and nine times in Luke. Luke's concept, usage and understanding of the term repentance differed with Mark and Matthew. This can be traced to their worldview and background. Mark's and Mathew's understanding of repentance is from the concept of repentance in Judaism. Horst Balz and Gerhard Schneider posits here that

> In early Judaism repentance was overwhelmingly understood as a return to the law and was often regarded as a prerequisite for holiness. Nevertheless, neither this understanding nor the stronger individualistic and, in part, casuistic orientation of the concept of repentance warrants the suspicion that it entails legalism (M. Limbeck, Die Ordnung des hails [1971]; Fiedler); rather, the parenetic objective should be kept in view. Moreover, early Judaism shows at least in principle that both the law and repentance were gifts of God's grace (Wisdom 11:23; 12:10, 19; Pr Man 8; the fifth of the eighteen benedictions). The concept of repentance acquired a special significance in the Qumram sect, whose members designated themselves the repentant ones of Israel.[9]

Luke's understanding of repentance is connected to the forgiveness of sins, as Horst Balz and Gerhard Schneider posit that:

> characteristic of the Lukan understanding of repentance is its connection with the forgiveness of sins (Acts 2:38, 3:19, 5:31, 8:22, 26:18 & 20, cf. Luke 3:3, 24:47) or with baptism and the reception of salvation. The revelation can be defined as follows: repentance is the precondition for forgiveness, which in turn is the prerequisite for receiving salvation (Acts 2:38, 3:19, cf. 8:22). This usage of *metavoeo,* supplemented occasionally by – *epistrepho* (3:19, 26:20, cf. Luke 17:4), shows that Luke understood repentance differently… influenced by Greek usage. Luke understand the term as the change of attitude

---

[8] Morris, *New Testament Theology*, 1990: 214.
[9] Horst Balz and Gerhard Schneider (ed), *Exegetical Dictionary of the New Testament.* Grand Rapids, Michigan, William B. Eerdmans Publishing Company,©1990. All rights reserved. Accessed through the PC Study Bible, version 5.

that leads to conversion, which must be followed, however, by corresponding deeds (Acts 26:20, cf. Luke 3:7). Nevertheless, Luke remains true to the traditional biblical heritage in that he views repentance as a once-and-for-all act (the only exception being the anthropological tendency of Luke 17:3f).[10]

Luke's understanding and usage of repentance in his gospel presents a room for the gentiles to gain the forgiveness of their sins and salvation if they repent of their sins.

Mark's presentation of Jesus demanding repentance from the people he preached to was different from the way Luke presented Jesus' demand of repentance. For example, in Mark 1:15 and many other passages, Balz and Schneider observed that Mark presented Jesus as demanding:

Repentance in response to the announcement of the reign of God and thus properly represents the structural uniqueness of Jesus' concept of repentance. New is the connection between faith and the gospel. Repentance therefore acquires the sense of the beginning of a turning toward Christian faith (cf. Mark 6:12, redactional). Correspondingly, Mark eliminates the concept of judgment from the preaching of repentance by John (the 'one who prepares the way'). The 'baptism of repentance for the forgiveness of sins' in Mark 1:4 are understood primarily as preparation and cleansing for Jesus' message of salvation.[11]

Luke, on the other hand, in Luke 13:3,5; 10:13; 11:32 and many other passages presented Jesus as demanding repentance vocatively from his hearers, as the failure to do so will bring judgment, just the way John the Baptist did.

Jesus' preaching of repentance alongside john the Baptist as a way out of escaping the judgment of God presented the urgency of repentance in a simplest form to the gentiles than the presentation of repentance in Mark and Matthew. This is because Luke's account combined john the Baptist's concept of repentance as a no return to the former things and lifestyle and a return to Yahweh with Jesus' imperative demand of repentance which required a commitment to the words and deeds of Jesus (Luke 10:13, 1:32). This presented a good

---

[10] Horst Balz and Gerhard Schneider (ed), *Exegetical Dictionary of the New Testament*. ©1990. All rights reserved.
[11] Horst Balz and Gerhard Schneider (ed), *Exegetical Dictionary of the New Testament*. ©1990. All rights reserved.

picture of repentance that "with Jesus it meant to live in the light of announced and already present salvation of the kingdom of God, which absolves all former guilt."[12]

In the story of the calling of Levi, all the three gospels were in agreement of Jesus response to the Pharisees and teachers of laws question, "way do you eat and drink with tax collectors and sinners?" Jesus response was, "it is not the healthy who need a doctor, but the sick. I have not come to call the righteous but sinners." Only Luke gave the addition "to repentance" Luke 5:32. Jesus' imperative demand for repentance which he commended his disciples to do likewise as presented by Luke can be seen in his disciples' and other apostles' preaching on repentance in the book of Acts 8:22, 2:38, 17:30, 26:20, 1:18 etc.

Background of the Book of Luke

Authorship

Early tradition, verified by second-century witnesses and the early title of the book favors Luke, the traveling companion of Paul, as the author of the books of Luke and Acts of the apostles. Although the case for Luke's use of medical language has been exaggerated, there is some evidence for it, and it is consonant with the tradition of Lukan authorship.

Location and date

Pertaining the date Luke wrote his gospel, there are a number of dates that have been suggested for the writing of Luke. Some suggest AD 60. But some still argues that if "Acts were written before the time of Nero's persecution (A.D 64)-which seems evident by the fact that Acts closed with Paul still alive and in prison- then the book of Luke must have been written several years before that, for Acts was subsequent to Luke. Though it is impossible to pinpoint a specific date, a time of composition between AD 58 and AD 60 fits well."[13] There is no clue as to where Luke wrote his gospel, some suggest that it is either Caesarea or Rome.

---

[12] Horst Balz and Gerhard Schneider (ed), *Exegetical Dictionary of the New Testament.* ©1990. All rights reserved.

[13] Horst Balz and Gerhard Schneider (ed), *Exegetical Dictionary of the New Testament.* ©1990. All rights reserved.

Message and purpose

Luke, in the literary prologue of the gospel presented two purposes in writing this book. "One was to confirm the faith of Theophilus, that is, to show that his faith in Christ rested on firm historical fact (1:3-4). His other purpose was to present Jesus as the Son of Man, who had been rejected by Israel. Because of this rejection, Jesus was also preached to Gentiles so that they could know the kingdom program of God and attain salvation."[14]

Conclusion

The relationship between Christians and Muslims today in Nigeria is not cordial. To some extent, it is more severe than the relationship between the Jews and gentiles before and during Jesus' time. The Jews then saw themselves as the only beneficiaries of God's redemptive plan and salvation. They did all within their reach to prevent the gospel from going to the gentiles, as the refusal of the disciples to go out of Jerusalem to preach the gospel to the surrounding gentile nations, the surprise of the disciples at seeing Jesus talking to the Samaritan woman by the well in Samaria, the refusal of the Jews to pass through Samaria to Galilee and many other proofs. The relationship between the Jews and the gentiles then was characterized y hatred. The Jews hated the gentiles probably because God used them to punished and deal with the Jews severally, and at the same time the gentiles were ruling over them. The Jews anticipated the coming of the messiah in the political aspect more than the spiritual aspect, i.e. to set them free from their Gentile rulers and establish a kingdom where they will have the right and opportunity to be governed and ruled by themselves more than the spiritual salvation and redemption the messiah will offer.

The relationship between Christians and Muslims in Nigeria today has negatively affected the Christians from performing their evangelistic mandate. The various attacks on Christians and the various appraisal attacks by the Christians have affected the relationship between Christians and Muslims thereby making it very difficult to fulfill the great commission and commandment of evangelizing/discipling the all nations and loving ones neighbor as oneself.

---

[14] Horst Balz and Gerhard Schneider (ed), *Exegetical Dictionary of the New Testament.* ©1990. All rights reserved.

Bibliography

Ronald A. Beers (Ed.), *New Living Translation Life Application Study Bible.* Carol Steam, Illinois, Tyndale House Publishers, Inc., 2007.

John A. Martin, "Luke," in the *Bible Knowledge Commentary: New Testament.*(eds., Walvoord, John F. and Zuck, Roy B.), Cook communications ministries, 2000. Accessed through the PC Study Bible, version 5.

Leon Morris, *New Testament Theology,* Grand Rapids, Michigan, Zondervan Publishing House, 1990.

Horst Balz and Gerhard Schneider (ed), *Exegetical Dictionary of the New Testament.* Grand Rapids, Michigan, William B. Eerdmans Publishing Company,©1990. All rights reserved. Accessed through the PC Study Bible, version 5.

Marshall I. Howard, *the gospel of Luke.* Exeter, the paternoster press, 1978.

Beers, Ronald A (ed), *new living translation life application study bible,* carol steam, Illinois, Tyndale house publishers, inc, 2007.

YOUR KNOWLEDGE HAS VALUE

- We will publish your bachelor's and master's thesis, essays and papers

- Your own eBook and book - sold worldwide in all relevant shops

- Earn money with each sale

Upload your text at www.GRIN.com and publish for free